TUDOR POWER AND GLORY

HENRY VIII AND THE FIELD OF CLOTH OF GOLD

Keith Dowen and Scot Hurst

ROYAL=ARMOURIES

Witness | Guardian | Expert | Leader

Published by Royal Armouries Museum, Armouries Drive, Leeds LS10 1LT, United Kingdom

www.royalarmouries.org

ISBN 978 1 91301 300 4

Edited by Martyn Lawrence

Designed by Riverside Publishing Solutions Ltd

Printed by Jellyfish Print Solutions

10 9 8 7 6 5 4 3 2 1

A CIP record for this book is available from the British Library

Every effort has been made to trace the copyright holders of images, where applicable. Any errors or omissions are unintentional, and the publisher will be pleased to insert any appropriate acknowledgements in future editions.

Contents

Introduction

The Field of Cloth of Gold, held in north-western France near the English enclave of Calais in June 1520, was an extravagant display of princely magnificence. Designed to consolidate the recent peace between England and France, representatives from both nations engaged in a spectacular demonstration of 'competitive hospitality' centred on a grand tournament involving jousting, tourneys and foot combat. Immortalised in works of art and eye-witness accounts, the Field of Cloth of Gold – so named because of the lavishness of the materials used – was one of the most opulent diplomatic and sporting events ever staged.

Field of Cloth of Gold

This interpretation of the Field of Cloth of Gold (dated 1545) depicts a number of key individuals, places and events. Henry VIII can be seen three times: riding into Guînes, meeting Francis I and watching the joust. © Royal Collection Trust / Her Majesty Queen Elizabeth II 2020

Background

Since his accession to the throne in 1509, Henry VIII had been determined to transform England from the somewhat insular country of his father into a modern, outward-looking European state. Aged 29 in 1520, Henry was in the prime of life. Extolled as 'rich, ferocious and thirsting for glory', he was cultured, pious and athletic – the very image of the ideal Renaissance ruler. The French king Francis I shared similar qualities. Praised as the 'perfect French gentleman', the 25-year-old Francis was energetic and ambitious. Determined to enhance his (and France's) reputation, Francis' recent Italian military campaigns had brought a level of personal glory on the battlefield that Henry eyed enviously.

Henry VIII

Aged 29 at the Field of Cloth of Gold, Henry VIII was young, ambitious and determined to establish himself on the European stage. © National Portrait Gallery

For the two young kings, the Field of Cloth of Gold not only provided the perfect opportunity to display the wealth of their respective courts, it also served to demonstrate the vast resources each king was able to command. For Henry, eager to revive the English glories of the Hundred Years War and erase memories of the brutal Wars of the Roses, the occasion was intended to firmly establish the Tudors as a leading European power. His early campaigns against France had been of little strategic value, despite the later boasts made by his government. The Battle of the Spurs (16 August 1513), for example, was played up as a great victory because Henry felt he had something to prove against a successful front-line commander. In reality it was little more than a minor skirmish, and Henry maintained a safe distance from the fighting.

Francis I

Only a few years younger than Henry, Francis had established himself as one of the most powerful rulers in Europe. This portrait from around 1530 shows Francis in his mid thirties. © The Louvre

The Battle of the Spurs

The Battle of the Spurs was portrayed as a great
military victory by the English. © Royal Collection
Trust / Her Majesty Queen Elizabeth II 2020

By 1514 Henry's allies, Holy Roman Emperor Maximilian I and Ferdinand II of Spain, had tired of war and made a separate peace with France. This forced the reluctant Henry, now running desperately short on funds, to follow suit. The subsequent Anglo-French treaty was cemented by the marriage of Henry's sister, Mary Tudor, to the ailing King Louis XII. The treaty also made provision for a future peace summit between the kings of England and France.

The political landscape within Europe soon shifted considerably. When Louis XII died in 1515, Francis I was crowned King of France. Soon afterwards, Charles I succeeded Ferdinand II as king of Spain, and following the death of Maximilian I in 1519, was also crowned Emperor Charles V of the Holy Roman Empire. Two vast competing powers had suddenly appeared. From his vantage point across the Channel, Henry was determined to establish himself as an equal and England as the third major power in Christendom.

The Negotiations

Selim I

Ottoman sultan Selim I (reigned 1512–20) who oversaw
a period of Islamic expansion into Eastern Europe.

Pope Leo X

Pope Leo X, who sought to unite Christian Europe
against the Ottoman threat. © Uffizi Gallery

Amidst this tense backdrop, there were calls for peace and unity from Pope Leo X. He sought to unite the Christian states of Europe in the face of aggressive Ottoman expansion, which had been creeping relentlessly westward under Selim I. Cardinal Thomas Wolsey, one of Henry VIII's foremost advisors, quickly seized upon the Pope's plan for a temporary five-year peace. Wolsey saw an opportunity to place himself at the heart of European politics by establishing Henry as the arbiter of European security.

By the 16th century, prominent humanist thinkers such as Erasmus and Thomas More were championing the virtues of peace over war. The strength of a prince was no longer measured purely by his ability to wage war, they argued, but also by his ability to make peace. The Universal Peace of 1518 was founded upon these principals. It brought together the leading twenty Christian states of Europe in a permanent non-aggression pact, the foremost signatories of which were England, France and the Holy Roman Empire. A second, parallel treaty between England and France was also signed, confirming their earlier commitment to peace. Once again, the alliance was cemented through a proposal of marriage, this time of the two-year-old daughter of Henry VIII, Princess Mary, to the one-year old Dauphin of France.

Erasmus of Rotterdam

Known as the 'Prince of Humanists', Erasmus was one of the foremost scholars of the Renaissance. © National Gallery

Having renewed and reinforced the earlier 1514 Anglo-French treaty, fresh interest in a summit emerged. On the surface, the meeting was an opportunity to celebrate the lasting peace through feats of arms and regal extravagance. There were, however, ulterior motives: both Henry and Francis knew that such flamboyant displays of wealth and power could only strengthen their personal standing.

The consolidation of French power and the establishment of English influence within Europe had tremendous repercussions for the balance of power on the continent. Charles V of the Holy Roman Empire was not ignorant of this, and even attempted to intervene personally. Immediately prior to Henry's departure for Calais, Charles visited England in a brazen attempt to upset the diplomatic process and either postpone or prevent the summit from taking place altogether. Guided by Wolsey, Henry trod a careful path courting both Francis and Charles as potential allies.

Sir Thomas More

A friend of Erasmus and a proponent of Humanist thought, Sir Thomas More accompanied Henry to the Field of Cloth of Gold. © The Frick Collection

WOLSEY.

The Field of Cloth of Gold therefore represented the culmination, but by no means the end, of years of difficult negotiation between England and France. Once the agreement for a peace summit was made, ambassadors in both courts worked tirelessly to bring the competitive kings together on equal terms. It was a near-impossible task for Cardinal Thomas Wolsey and Sir Richard Wingfield, the English diplomats to whom the task fell.

Wolsey had spent almost six years working towards the summit. Alongside establishing Henry as an indispensable figure in European politics, he also sought to further his own ambitions, positioning himself as chief architect of peace and – as cardinal – a leading candidate for the papacy. His presence at many key moments of the summit, such as the closing mass of peace over which he presided, gave him the perfect opportunity to further his objectives. Wingfield was an experienced courtier who had been appointed Lord Deputy of Calais in 1511 and ambassador to France in 1520. Successfully steering a difficult course between the competing interests of Henry, Francis and Emperor Charles V, he was a crucial figure in securing the arrangements for the Field of Cloth of Gold. During his tenure as ambassador Wingfield developed a close personal relationship with the French king, gaining a level of unfettered access that often broke with traditional protocol.

Cardinal Thomas Wolsey

Cardinal Thomas Wolsey was Henry's most trusted advisor, leading both the negotiations and preparations for the Field of Cloth of Gold. © Trinity College Cambridge

Henricus dei gracia Rex Anglie et Francie et dominus hibernie Universis et singulis presentes litteras inspecturis

The diplomatic skills of Wolsey and Wingfield were often tested, as both Henry and Francis sought to establish themselves as *primus inter pares* (first amongst equals). Consequently, much of the negotiation was focused on achieving a veneer of parity between the two kings, while at the same time subtly indulging their egos and ambitions. Henry desired prestige and a central position in European politics; Francis needed an ally against the Holy Roman Empire and consolidation of his own existing position. Of the two, Henry faced the greater challenge, since France had long been at the forefront of art, fashion, modern military thinking and scholarship. The Field of Cloth of Gold was the perfect opportunity to present England as a formidable modern force.

Treaty Documents

Documents preparing the ground for Henry and Francis to meet. Above: the request, dated 1518; below: the agreement to attend the summit, dated 1520.
© The National Archives / Archives Nationales de France

Greenwich and the Development of the Armourer's Craft

The Renaissance was renowned for its outstanding artistic achievements. It was an age when men of wealth actively encouraged artists and craftsmen to give full rein to their creativity, resulting in paintings and sculptures of incredible beauty. Armour likewise reached new heights of sophistication. Far from merely serving a defensive purpose, a suit of armour was also a visual art form, expressing the wealth and status of the wearer. Artistic patronage upheld social status in a deeply hierarchical society, a point of crucial importance in a changing world.

POTENTISSIMVS · MAXIMVS · ET · INVICTISSIMVS · CÆSAR · MAXIMILIANVS
QVI · CVNCTOS · SVI · TEMPORIS · REGES · ET · PRINCIPES · IVSTICIA · PRVDENCIA
MAGNANIMITATE · LIBERALITATE · PRÆCIPVE · VERO · BELLICA · LAVDE · ET
ANIMI · FORTIDVDINE · SVPERAVIT · NATVS · EST · ANNO · SALVTIS · HVMANÆ
M · CCCC · LIX · DIE · MARCII · IX · VIXIT · ANNOS · LIX · MENSES · IX · DIES · XXV
DECESSIT · VERO · ANNO · M · D · XIX · MENSIS · IANVARII · DIE · XII · QVEM · DEVS
OPT · MAX · IN · NVMERVM · VIVENCIVM · REFERRE · VELIT ·

Holy Roman Emperor Maximilian I

This idealised portrait of Maximilian by Albrecht Dürer proclaims him as the
'Very Most Powerful and Inviolable Emperor'. Maximilian is shown holding a
pomegranate, his personal badge. © Kunsthistorisches Museum

Weisskunig Armoury

This depiction of Maximilian's court armoury at Innsbruck shows the Emperor engaging with his master armourer Conrad Seusenhofer. Henry's armourers at Greenwich used identical tools. From Hans Burgkmair's *Der Weisskunig* (1516).

Of all the patrons of the armourer's art, the Holy Roman Emperor Maximilian I was one of the greatest. Having succeeded his uncle as Archduke of the Tyrol in 1490, the future emperor established his main residence at Innsbruck. Although a workshop producing high-quality armour already existed in neighbouring Mühlau, Maximilian opened his own personal court armoury at Innsbruck in 1504. Staffed with salaried workers, free of restrictive working conditions and with Maximilian's direct input, the Innsbruck armourers established themselves as trend-setters, producing some of the most beautiful and technologically-accomplished armours ever made. Determined to attract leading armourers to his workshop, Maximilian employed the Augsburg master armourer Conrad Seusenhofer, who was made head of the court armoury a few years later. Beyond his personal requirements, Maximilian commissioned pieces for family members as well as foreign rulers and dignitaries. Fully appreciative of the value such diplomatic gifts had as a means of cementing alliances, strengthening friendship and conveying the magnificence of his court, Maximilian ensured Innsbruck became the preeminent centre for the production of presentation armours. His success would inspire others to do the same.

Although geographically and politically on the periphery of Europe, England had a long history of armour production: in the 15th century, English armour had developed its own distinct identity and many powerful men, including members of the royal household, patronised English armourers. However, the kings of England did not possess their own dedicated court armoury, and it was not until Henry VIII's accession that the country was set on a new course. Wishing to create a modern European-style court in England, Henry employed numerous foreign craftsmen – painters, sculptors, musicians, glaziers and tapestry-makers. He also looked abroad for armourers. Whilst the standard of English armour was certainly high, Henry considered it too conservative and provincial for his cosmopolitan tastes. It hindered his ability to engage on equal terms in diplomatic gift-giving.

Before his accession, Henry had been greatly impressed by Maximilian's son, the 28-year-old Archduke Philip of Burgundy, who had spent two months at the English court. A skilled jouster, Philip brought fine armours with him during his stay in England. Having seen the output of the best Continental armourers at first hand, it was no surprise that Henry's gaze was directed towards Europe. Initially, he looked to Milan and Brussels, both highly-esteemed centres of armour production. In March 1511 he contracted the Milanese armourers Filippo de Grampis, Giovanni Angela de Littis (and three other unnamed Italian masters) for a period of two years. Later that same year the Flemish armourers Peter Fevers and Jacob 'Copyn' de Watte, together with their assistants, also entered Henry's service. Like Maximilian at Innsbruck, Henry took a great interest in

Armet

Made by Maximillian's highly-skilled court armourer Conrad Seusenhofer, the elaborate fluting or ridges on this helmet took great skill to achieve. Such pieces inspired Henry to establish his own court armoury in England. IV.412

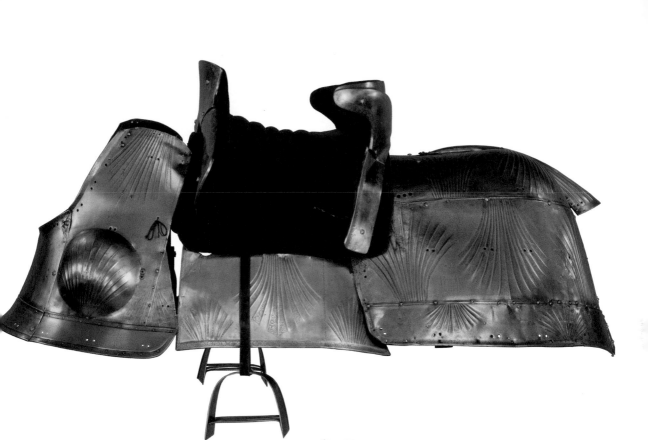

'Italian' Bard

Comprising a peytral, crupper, one flanchard and a pair of stirrups (the saddle steels do not belong), the surface of the metal has been embossed with flutes and etched gilt foliage interspersed with the Tudor badges of the rose and portcullis. VI.14-16

the work of his armourers and situated his court armoury adjacent to his favourite palace at Greenwich. It may have been during this first phase of the workshop that Henry's Italian armourers produced the 'Italian' bard (so named due to the 'Italianate' nature of the decoration) in the Royal Armouries collection. Although the payment records are incomplete, it appears that the Italian armourers did not stay at Greenwich beyond their two-year contract, although other Milanese armours continued to be employed until at least 1559. The reason for their apparent departure is not clear, but may have been the result of Henry's increasingly close ties with Maximilian.

Burgundian Bard

Originally gilded, the bard has been embossed with the crossed branches and fire-steels of the prestigious knightly Order of the Golden Fleece. The pomegranates may be a reference to Maximilian's personal badge. VI.6-12

Greenwich Tools

In September 1511 the armoury was equipped with a variety of tools and equipment to the value of £13 including stakes, shears, hammers, chisels and punches. XVIII.97; 1626; 830; 98; 1624; 1627; 1628; 1625

Looking to strengthen his European alliances, particularly against the French, Maximilian's interest in English affairs had begun during the reign of Henry VII. Although the relationship between the two rulers soured, ties between Maximilian and England improved following the accession of Henry VIII in 1509. Consequently, it may have been at this time that Henry was presented with the 'Burgundian Bard'. Fashioned by the Brussels armourer Guillem Margot and decorated by the goldsmith Paul van Vrelant sometime between *c*.1505 and *c*.1514, the bard was probably originally made for either Maximilian or his son Philip. Despite being 'second hand', the bard was a clear indication of Maximilian's regard for his English counterpart.

Horned Helmet

The curious 'Horned Helmet' is the only surviving element of Maximilian's gift armour. Originally it was embellished with fretted silver-gilt plates laid over velvet, of which only the recessed panels and the rivet holes for their attachment on the skull remain. IV.22

Foot Combat Armour

Like the Foot Combat armour of Henry VIII, this armour of c.1515 features numerous articulating lames designed to protect vulnerable parts of the body. Although elaborately decorated this armour was designed to fulfil a practical defensive role on the tournament field. © Musée de l'Armée

Hoping to ensure Henry's friendship in the ever-shifting sands of Renaissance Europe, in 1511 the emperor instructed Conrad Seusenhofer to produce a richly-decorated gift armour for Henry. At the same time Henry also commissioned two additional armours for himself, both of which appear to have arrived with Maximilian's gift in 1514. Probably the finest armour ever seen in England, it was no coincidence that the following year Henry engaged the services of armourers from within the Holy Roman Empire. Known as 'Almains' ('Almain' being an archaic word for 'German-speaking' or 'Germany'), they were servants of the Crown and were therefore only permitted to make armours for Henry or others who had obtained a royal warrant. Initially based at Greenwich, Henry's armourers moved to Southwark in 1516 to facilitate work on the armoury complex, and did not return until building was complete in 1520. It was during this period of upheaval that the Almains, under the direction of master armourer Martin van Royne/de

Prone, produced two foot combat armours for Henry VIII.

Designed to be worn by Henry at the Field of Cloth of Gold, the creation of all-enclosing foot combat armour was a technical masterpiece. It was also a personal triumph for Henry who proved his armourers could compete with the best in Europe. Frustratingly it was never worn. Only three months before the tournament, the French changed the rules, and work on the armour came to a halt.

Foot Combat Armour

One of only four of this type surviving, and a remarkable piece of engineering, this foot combat armour was designed to fully encase the body in steel plate. It comprised 235 separate parts with a sophisticated system of sliding rivets and internal leather straps. II.6

The Preparations

The Field of Cloth of Gold was a monumental logistical undertaking. It involved a labour force of several thousand and cost more than each country usually spent on their courts in a year. Such was the scale of the event and the investment of time, men, money and resources that a genuine commitment towards peace from both sides should be acknowledged.

It was imperative that both kings were seen to have contributed equally to the summit. Neither wanted to be outdone, nor appear to intentionally outdo the other, and diplomats on both sides were at pains to ensure parity. While both committed roughly the same towards financing the event, Henry's annual revenue was far lower than that of Francis, placing a much greater burden upon his coffers. He was clearly prepared to pay handsomely for the privilege of establishing himself as an equal on the European stage.

Both kings sought to surround themselves with impressive retinues. Again, this was more of a challenge for Henry. In 1520, the population of England was 2.5 million, compared with France's 15 million, and Francis had much more latitude to select the best and brightest to accompany him to the summit. To match the size of the French entourage, Henry was forced to invite almost all the higher English peerage as well as a sizeable proportion of the gentry. This included many low-ranking knights and nobles with little personal wealth or status. While the numbers of attendees were roughly equal (about 6,000 on each side) the humble origins of many amongst Henry's retinue – including key figures such as Cardinal Wolsey and the Duke of Suffolk – did not escape the notice or the mockery of the French. The individual costs involved would also have been considerable, particularly for the lower-ranked, but it is unlikely that anyone would have declined Henry's 'request' to attend. It would have been an honour and a duty to represent the sovereign, as well as an ideal opportunity for personal advancement.

Invitations to the summit were issued two months before the event.

The only surviving invitation was addressed to Sir Adrian Fortescue, a relatively minor official knighted in 1503 when Henry was Prince of Wales. Amongst other details, the document issued instructions regarding appropriate dress, reminding participants that as representatives of England, their clothing should be appropriate to their station. It also specified that the size of each retinue was dependent upon the status of the individual. A separate memorandum drafted in 1520 gives a complete breakdown of the English entourage and the composition of each rank's retinue. It specified that earls in the king's entourage were required to bring two chaplains and thirty other persons, six being gentlemen, with twenty horses. Knights were required to bring twelve servants, one of whom was to be a chaplain, and eight horses. In Fortescue's invitation, he was specifically ordered to attend as part of Queen Katherine's entourage, along with 'ten tall personages well and conveniently apparailled for this purposed'. Intriguingly, his invitation contradicted the formal memorandum, requiring only ten 'personages' rather than the twelve men and eight horses otherwise stated.

Sir Adrian Fortescue

Sir Adrian Fortescue participated in Henry VIII's 1513 campaign. He was executed in 1539 for treason and was beatified in the 19th century as a Roman Catholic martyr. © Collegio di San Paolo

Another prominent attendee was Sir Giles Capel, a close friend of Henry VIII who had been knighted during the 1513 campaign. Capel not only accompanied Henry during his first meeting with Francis, but also competed alongside the king during the joust. Though no lists survive of those who participated in the foot combat, it is possible that Capel did take part. A foot combat helm associated with his tomb (in Rayne, Essex) survives and matches the type worn during the foot combat.

Capel Helm

This great bascinet for the foot combat, dating to *c.*1510 is associated with the tomb of Sir Giles Capel. One of the finest examples of its kind, this is representative of the helms likely to have been used at the barriers during the Field of Cloth of Gold. © The Metropolitan Museum of Art

The tournament itself was to take place in neutral territory between the English outpost of Guînes and the French town of Ardes. This would, in theory, ensure further parity between the two monarchs. However, before the kings and their 12,000 followers descended upon the Val d'Or, extensive preparations were required. Francis entrusted the French preparations to Gaspard de Coligny, Marshal of France, and Jacques Ricard de Genouillac, Great Master of the Royal Artillery. Given the scale of the task, the logistical experience of the Royal Artillery proved invaluable. Not only did the French encampment need constructing, but the town of Ardes – destroyed by the English in 1513 – required extensive repairs. The walls were reinforced, accommodation for Francis was prepared and a grand banqueting house constructed within the town. The presence of a French artillery company also enabled military reinforcement of the region: despite the recent peaceful overtures, the long history of animosity between England and France had left a lingering sense of mistrust. Garrisons were increased, walls strengthened, and arms and armour for around 2,000 Frenchmen supplied to nearby towns. Equally suspicious, the English followed suit, shipping artillery from the Tower wharf across to Calais.

The Embarkation

In this painting Henry is shown departing aboard the *Great Harry*, rigged with golden sails. In reality it is likely he travelled in the smaller but more luxurious *Katherine Plesaunce*. © Royal Collection Trust / Her Majesty Queen Elizabeth II 2020

Under the charge of the earl of Worcester, who answered directly to Wolsey, most of the core English work centred upon the construction of the lists and a temporary palace for Henry. 3,000 workers were contracted. The temporary palace, located immediately outside the castle of Guînes, has endured as one of the iconic features of the Field of Cloth of Gold. Though descriptions of the structure vary, it apparently covered almost 10,000 square metres and was made up of four wings with a central courtyard. Each wall was one hundred metres long and consisted of a brick base two metres high, topped with canvas walls supported by a wooden frame and painted to look like stonework. 150 bricklayers, 250 carpenters, 100 joiners, 30 pairs of sawyers, 40 plasterers, 50 glazers and 24 painters were involved in the work, and contemporaries claimed that even the great Leonardo da Vinci could not have devised a more spectacular structure. The castle at Guînes was also renovated and reinforced, not for any military or strategic purpose, but rather that it was deemed, 'unfit to be seen'. Finally, the mill from the Greenwich armoury was temporarily dismantled, shipped across the Channel and erected in Guînes for the duration of the tournament, for which a team of just four labourers and three carpenters were hired. Four forges were also either requisitioned or constructed nearby, alongside a central makeshift armoury established within the Great Wool-house in Calais.

In the negotiations prior to the event, it had been agreed that England would source and supply arms for the tournament. Sir Edward Guildford travelled throughout Europe sourcing materials, arms and armour. Most of the horses were obtained from France, the Low Countries and Italy, but included several imperial gifts from Charles V which arrived from Spain. A wide variety of essential objects were sourced by Guildford and his agents and was stored in the Great Wool-house in Calais:

1,000 Milanese swords

2,000 counter-rondels

1,000 vamplates from Innsbruck

600 two-handed swords

100 heavy swords for the tourney on horseback

600 files

500 chisels

500 punches

3 packs of rivets containing 1,200 each

12 shaffrons

The lists (the arena in which tournament events took place) were around 270 metres long by 100 metres wide, with galleries for spectators along each side, triumphal arches at each end and accommodation within for the kings to arm and rest. They lists were initially planned to be within neutral terrain but were later relocated to a new site within English territory, equidistant from English Guînes and French Ardes. Henry demanded this change to reflect the risks he was taking by crossing the sea to France, a decision that Sir Richard Wingfield eventually convinced the French to accept.

In return for ceding ground, the French negotiated oversight of the tournament rules, and it was here, in the eye of this colossal logistical storm, that a major last-minute change was made. Francis insisted on a 'clarification' to the rules of the foot combat, specifying the need for a tonlet armour instead of a (battle)field armour with pieces of advantage. Unhappily, this rendered Henry's spectacular new all-enclosing harness useless. The armourers at Greenwich were required to produce a completely new armour in barely three months. This itself was not impossible, but by the time it was communicated many men, tools and materials were en-route to Calais.

Tonlet Armour

Despite the difficult circumstances of its construction and composite nature, the tonlet armour is a testament to the skills and ingenuity of the Greenwich armourers. II.7

Artist's impression

An artist's impression of Henry's tonlet armour.
© Michael Perry

Henry's reaction to the change is not documented but he appears not to have formally disputed the decision. Ultimately, the armourers only produced the skirt and pauldrons from scratch, and the rest of the armour was gathered from existing pieces to create a composite harness. Although the creation of the tonlet was a huge compromise, in terms of both circumstance and construction, few at the tournament would have immediately noticed. The new armour was luxuriously decorated with a blued and gilt checkerboard pattern, which helped to conceal many of its imperfections. In the end, despite the mistakes and compromises that went into its construction, the tonlet is a testament to the consummate ingenuity of Henry's Greenwich armourers.

The Feat of Arms

The Field of Cloth of Gold was first and foremost a feat of arms, or *'pas d'armes'*. It provided the ideal arena for the English and French to demonstrate their knightly skills amidst the wider diplomatic work at hand. As a celebratory occasion, the role of tournaments in promoting cordial relations had long been established. During the Hundred Years War (1337-1453), tournaments regularly marked periods of peace between England and France. Indeed, in the lead up to the Field of Cloth of Gold the Admiral of France, Guillaume Guffier, wrote to Charles Brandon, Duke of Suffolk stating that there was no more honest pastime to show all the friendship between the two princes. Yet for all the peaceful overtures, beneath the demonstrations of chivalry on the tournament field lurked an implicit warning: military force could be used if diplomacy failed.

Dramatic and spectacular, the tournament was an expression of wealth and power, a piece of visual propaganda designed to impress both combatants and spectators. The Tudor historian Edward Hall vividly described how competitors at the Field of Cloth of Gold wore rich clothing over their armour whilst their horses were equipped with decorative trappings. Henry and Francis wore costly fabrics woven with gold and silver, elaborately embroidered with symbols conveying their personal character and aspirations. Henry's designs were more nationalistic, proclaiming his – and England's glories – whilst Francis chose more complex philosophical themes.

Over the seventeen days of the summit, the formal combats at the Field of Cloth of Gold comprised eight days of jousting, two days of tourneying and two days of foot combat. Henry and Francis were the chief challengers or defenders (*tenans*) who, with a select group of men (made up of equal numbers of French and Englishmen), faced 200–300 answerers or comers (*venans*). (Greater numbers had been expected but the tension between Henry, Francis and Charles V meant that no one from the Holy Roman Empire answered the challenge.) A Tree of Honour stood at the end of the tiltyard. Erected on a mound encircled by a railing, the artificial tree was constructed from wood and costly fabrics, and entwined with the hawthorn (for England) and the raspberry (for France). Hung on its branches were three shields, each representing the different events: grey and black for the joust, gold and tawny for the tourney and silver for the foot combat. Prior to the tournament each of the *venans* touched the shields corresponding to the events in which they wished to participate, and their name was recorded by the heralds.

The rules of the tournament followed French custom. Although seemingly restrictive, the elaborate rules were designed to allow combatants to show their aggression and martial prowess whilst still maintaining a degree of safety. Lances were fitted with coronels while swords and spears were rebated or blunted. Danger, however, was always present, and even Francis suffered a minor injury during the joust.

David and Bathsheba

An anachronistic depiction of the story of David and Bathsheba. The luxurious fabrics worn over the armour are representative of those worn at the Field of Cloth of Gold. © Museum of the Renaissance, Écouen

The joust was the most prestigious event at any tournament. It required years of training, and enabled competitors to display skill, bravery and horsemanship. Given the ideal stage for heroic feats of arms, the jousters strove to win the favour of queens Claude and Katherine and the noble ladies present. Both Henry and Francis were accomplished jousters with Henry, ever the obsessive sportsman, probably the better of the two. Sadly neither Henry's nor Francis' armour survives nor is there much information to suggest where they might have been made.

Coronel

2,000 coronels were ordered for the joust at the Field of Cloth of Gold. The multi-pronged lance tip was designed to bite into armour or shield, spreading the force of the impact. VII.1543

Lalaing Joust

Shields were not used at the Field of Cloth of
Gold, but this depiction of a joust gives a good
impression of the equipment and jousting in 1520.
© The J. Paul Getty Museum, Los Angeles

Jousting began on Monday 11 June and lasted until the following Tuesday, although disappointingly rain halted proceedings on several occasions. Henry and Francis led 16 *tenans* whilst 145 *venans*, most of whom were French, were divided into 14 bands or teams, each comprising 10–12 men. Following the fashion at the French court, the jousters were instructed to wear armour for the (battle) field with additional reinforcing pieces, rather than more specialised tournament equipment. This decision may have had the additional benefit of attracting more participants to the Field, as fewer men were likely to own costly tournament armour. To ensure no one possessed an unfair advantage, heralds were on hand to see the rules were followed, whilst marshals maintained discipline during the feat of arms.

Field Harness

Made by the Italian armourer Niccolo Silva, this field armour has been fitted with reinforcing pieces, such as the large guard of the vambrace worn on the left arm. Silva may have supplied armour to the French court for the Field of Cloth of Gold. © Musée de l'Armée

Flemish Armet

Designed for the battlefield, this Flemish 'armet' matches those worn at the Field of Cloth of Gold. Lacking the more extensive protection found on specialised tournament helmets, various reinforcing pieces would have been worn. IV.576

Although it was spectacular, the joust at the Field of Cloth of Gold was not as successful as many hoped. High winds caused difficulties, and the relatively low number of hits appears to have been partly caused by the lack of counter-tilts or low barriers, which ran parallel to the central tilt. These were designed to create a channel down which the jousters would charge and keep the horses close to the central barrier. Their removal, at the insistence of the English, caused horses to swerve and made it harder for the jousters to hit their target. Nonetheless, Francis and Henry performed well, and often ran more than the prescribed eight (or usually five) courses. On one occasion, Henry hit with such force that he broke the visor pivot of his opponent's helmet.

With the jousts over, attention turned to the tourney. Fought in the open field, two against two, combatants were armed in field armour and equipped with lances and rebated swords. Simulating battlefield cavalry combat, the tourney enabled impressive displays of horsemanship and skilful swordplay. Over the two days Henry and Francis and their *tenans* competed against roughly fifty *venans*. On the second day Henry encountered Robert III de la Mark, maréchal de Fleuranges, and drove him back with such force that he broke the Frenchman's shoulder defence.

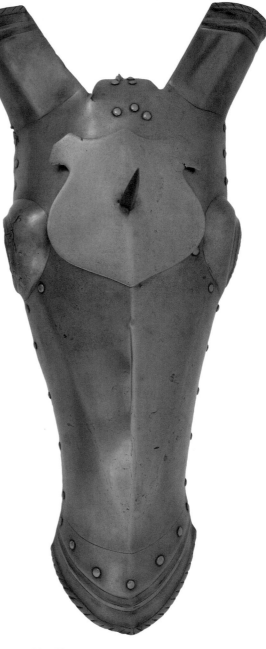

Jousting Cheque

This score cheque from the Field of Cloth of Gold features the names of the *tenans* and *venans* along with their heraldry including those of Henry and Francis. Scores have been recorded in the rectangular boxes. © Society of Antiquaries, London

Shaffron

Although the French rules did not specifically mention horse armour, it is likely that horses were protected by a steel shaffron to protect the head and a leather bard to protect the body. VI.68

The final event, on 22–23 June, was the combat on foot at the barriers. Originating from the judicial duel, the foot combat usually involved armoured competitors fighting inside an enclosure armed with a variety of weapons such as the sword, pollaxe and dagger. With the ever-present threat of serious injury, a horizontal barrier was introduced at the end of the 15th century to help separate combatants and try and ensure a certain level of safety. Nonetheless, despite these precautions, the foot combat remained a hazardous activity. With this in mind the barrier erected at the Field of Cloth of Gold was specially designed to incorporate a pair of side bars which could be swung open like a gate to force the combatants apart. Although the barrier was long enough to enable twenty men to stand along each side, the bouts were two against two. This was probably to ensure that combatants remained clearly visible to the spectators whilst also ensuring the fight did not descend into a brawl.

Pollaxe

A formidable weapon, the pollaxe had emerged in response to the development of more extensive plate armour, which had rendered swords less effective. Designed to cut, stab and crush armour, its use on the tournament field led to the development of more protective all-enclosing armour. VII.1510

Due to the political sensitivities surrounding the event, not to mention the risk of serious injury to Henry and Francis, pollaxes were not used at the Field of Cloth of Gold. According to the Tudor historian Edward Hall, the combat at the barriers was fought with single-handed swords, 'puncheon spears', two-handed swords and 'casting darts'. Francis had initially been opposed to the inclusion of two-handed swords, fearing that they would damage the competitors' gauntlets, whereas Henry favoured any weapon that showed his greater strength. In the end, a compromise was reached and two-handed swords were included as an optional event.

Sandricourt

Barriers were introduced to foot combat events in the late 15th century to keep contestants apart. However, in the heat of combat men often grappled over the barrier. © Bibliothèque Nationale de France

Spear

Unlike this sharp example, the casting and thrusting spears at the Field of Cloth of Gold were rebated for safety. VII.85

The combat at the barriers was divided into two phases. Initially the combatants fought with thrusting or 'puncheon' spears before moving on to single-handed swords. According to the Venetian eye-witness Marino Sanuto the fighting was so vigorous that even when the spears were broken men continued to beat each other with the stumps before hurling the remnants at each other. Single-handed swords were then brought to bear. Hall described how, with queens Katherine and Claude looking on, the two kings 'fought with such force that the fire sprang out of their armour'. The second phase of the contest was fought with casting darts or spears,

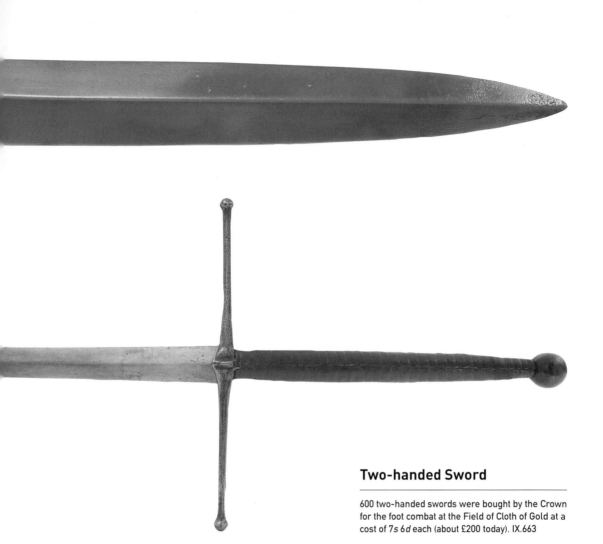

Two-handed Sword

600 two-handed swords were bought by the Crown for the foot combat at the Field of Cloth of Gold at a cost of 7s 6d each (about £200 today). IX.663

and two-handed swords. Sadly, very few details of the combat survive, and as one observer remarked, 'both Englishmen and Frenchmen fought well and with high spirits'.

After twelve days of combat the tournament drew to a close, and mass was celebrated by Cardinal Wolsey in a richly-decorated chapel specially erected on the tournament field. The following day, prizes were given: both kings received diamond and ruby rings whilst other champions received jewels, rings or collars. With one final meeting on the Monday, the extravagance of the Field of Cloth of Gold came to an end.

Tiltyard Diplomacy

Although the Field of Cloth of Gold was intended to be a celebration of peace and brotherhood, every moment was carefully choreographed. It was essential that Henry and Francis were able to present themselves at their most magnificent without appearing to overshadow one another. Throughout the tournament, traditional displays of chivalric and romantic ideals – often expressed through symbolic costume and elaborate ceremony – tempered the displays of aggression. The competitive theatricality of the tournament field provided the perfect environment for these public displays of skill and comradeship, while the banquets and masques enabled more personal and informal relationship-building.

Relief sculpture of the Field of Cloth of Gold

Depicting the first meeting between Henry VIII (on the left) and Francis I (on the right), this contemporary relief sculpture from the Hôtel de Bougtheroulde in Rouen gives an idea of the magnificence and scale of the event. © Alamy

Alongside the martial displays and ongoing diplomacy, the Field of Cloth of Gold was also an opportunity for Henry to present himself as a true Renaissance prince. This was achieved in part by his own outward appearance, but also by his choice of immediate companions and royal guard. The Yeomen of the Guard, established by Henry VII after the battle of Bosworth (1485), were both an elite fighting force and a

Treaty of 1527

The Yeomen of the Guard, shown on the right, were equipped with the finest arms, armour and clothing. © The National Archives

visual symbol of the power of their royal master. This was clear from their ostentatious appearance and the quality of their weapons and uniforms. Their captain, Sir Henry Marney, was commanded to bring two hundred of 'the tallest and most elect persons' of the Guard to the Field of Cloth of Gold. Evidently this had the desired effect as several French accounts detail their appearance in impressive detail.

Bill

Henry purchased beautifully-decorated arms and armour from Italy for his Yeomen of the Guard. Originally partly gilded, this bill was probably fitted with an expensive brazil-wood stave and embellished with velvet and silk in the Tudor colours of white and green.

Corseque

The staff of this winged spear (or corseque) features elaborate etched and gilt decoration incorporating fashionable Renaissance motifs, and may have originally been covered in red velvet. VII.1340

Longbow

Widely associated with England's victories over France during the Hundred Years War, the longbow, such as this example from the *Mary Rose*, had developed into a potent symbol of the nation's military greatness. XI.1

Gilt Buckler

Possibly made for Henry or a member of his guard, this unique gilded shield is etched in a similar style to Henry's tonlet armour. It features the coat of arms o' Henry VIII, the Tudor badge of the rose and portcullis and the pomegranate badge of Queen Katherine. © Musée de l'Armée

The meetings and encounters between Henry and Francis were carefully stage-managed by Cardinal Wolsey to eliminate any risk of diplomatic *faux pas* – a complex piece of live propaganda. There were, however, some unscripted moments that threatened to unravel Wolsey's hard work, as both kings playfully tested the limits of diplomacy. When rain prevented the joust from taking place on 13 June, 24 members of Henry's guard provided a display of their famed archery skills. Since English archers played a decisive role in several French defeats during the Hundred Years War, this innocuous display could have easily upset the friendly atmosphere that Wolsey sought to create. As it was, Francis was said to have been dismissive of the display, making 'but small countenance at that pastime'.

For his own part, Francis had a particular habit of disregarding convention. On the morning of 17 June, he barged his way into Henry's bedchamber unannounced and flamboyantly offered himself as a prisoner, much to the bewilderment of the half-dressed English king. Through such displays of aggressive comradeship, he personalised his formal relationship with Henry. However, this 'weaponised diplomacy' forced the English king to reciprocate in kind, as Francis subtly promoted himself as first amongst equals. Henry also tired of the endless formalities, prompting him on one occasion to get to grips with his French counterpart far more literally than Wolsey had ever anticipated. Although the kings had agreed to compete as brothers and never against each other, Henry chose to disregard protocol and challenged Francis to an impromptu wrestling match. Unfortunately, events did not go according to plan, as he was promptly thrown to the ground by the French king. This embarrassment could have very easily turned into a serious diplomatic episode, but in the end the good humour of the kings prevailed, and any upset was (at least publicly) averted.

Beneath the veneer of brotherhood and unity though, there

was a very real sense of tension. All present would have been painfully aware of just how recently England and France had been at war, with many participants on both sides being veterans of the 1513 campaign. So entrenched was the mistrust between the nations that even as the kings' retinues approached each other on the day of their meeting, there was a moment of pause. Both sides were wary of the possibility of betrayal. Little wonder that the Field of Cloth of Gold was so meticulously choreographed, and why the slightest misunderstanding could have enormous ramifications.

Charles V, Holy Roman Emperor

Emperor Charles V was deeply concerned that an Anglo-French alliance would upset the balance of power in Europe and threaten the dominance of the Holy Roman Empire. He sought an exclusive alliance with Henry against the French. © Museum of Fine Arts Budapest

Conclusion

By 1522, England and France were once again at war. Despite the years of planning, monumental logistical efforts and vast sums of money that went into making the Field of Cloth of Gold a reality, the fragile peace did not last. The looming threat of Charles V and the Holy Roman Empire made it impossible to cement a lasting Anglo-French union, even though both parties may have sincerely hoped that the tournament would cement new bonds of friendship.

Given how quickly war returned, it is tempting to believe that neither side genuinely intended to honour the Universal Peace. Did this mean that the Field of Cloth of Gold was little more than a sham? Far from it: the sheer expense and effort that went into the event suggests that it represented a genuine investment in the cause of peace. Ultimately,

the treaty was not broken because of any real failing in English foreign policy, nor because Henry courted both Charles V and Francis I as potential allies. The real failure was due to the irreconcilable tension that existed between Charles and Francis, which forced Henry to choose a side or find himself excluded again from European politics. By 1521 Henry had made his choice, negotiating a secret anti-French alliance with the Holy Roman Empire, and by 1522 his forces, under the command of the Duke of Suffolk, were once again rampaging through France. The Universal Peace, despite its humanist ideals and its promises of a new age of European brotherhood, lay in tatters.

Yet Henry was successfully positioned upon the European stage, and in the years to come would ensure his legacy as one of England's most influential rulers. The work of his Greenwich armourers became renowned throughout Europe. And England, just a generation after the Wars of the Roses, was emerging as a true Renaissance nation.

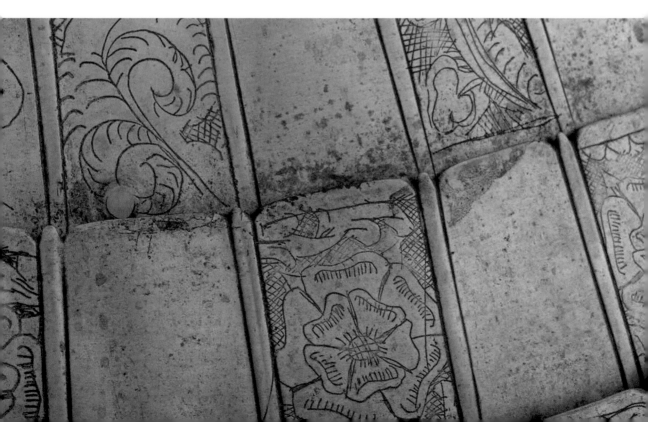

Acknowledgements

Thanks are due to Studio MB for exhibition design and Jonathan Chadwick for graphic design. Also we are grateful to Toby Capwell and Marina Viallon for help during the research and writing process; to Michael Perry for the superb illustration on page 41 and for additional advice; and to colleagues at the Royal Armouries for continued help throughout the project.